Francis Shoots Pool at Chubb's Bar

Poems by Al Ortolani

Kansas City Spartan Press Missouri

Spartan Press
Kansas City, Missouri
spartanpresskc.com

Spartan Press

Copyright © Al Ortolani, 2019
Second Edition
ISBN: 978-1-950380-44-2
LCCN: 2019943701

Design, edits and layout: Jeanette Powers, Jason Ryberg
Cover photos: Al Ortolani
Interior images: Phil Drake, Jeep Hunter
All rights reserved. No part of this publication may be reproduced or transmitted in any form or by any means, electronic or mechanical, including photocopying, recording or by info retrieval system, without prior written permission from the author

This book was originally published as part of the Prospero's POP Poetry series, which ran from 2015 through 2017.

Special thanks to Prospero's Books, Jeanette Powers, Will Leathem, Tom Wayne, M. Scott Douglass, Main Street Rag, Bert Fox, Maria David and The Charlotte Observer.

The poems in this book appeared—although sometimes in different versions—in the following journals and collections. The author would like to thank the editors for their support:

Ann Arbor Review, Bellowing Ark, The Buddhist Poetry Review, Camel Saloon, Front Porch Review, The Galway Review, I-70 Review, Light Year, Lummox, Melancholy Hyperbole, Metazen, The Orange Room Review, PresenceMag.com, The Rusty Truck, Turtle Island Quarterly, Eunoia (Hocked Gun Press), Wild Goose Poetry Review, Word Riot, Finding the Edge (Woodley Press), The Last Hippie of Camp 50 (Woodley Press), Waving Mustard in Surrender (New York Quarterly Books).

TABLE OF CONTENTS

Thursday Morning / 1

Before Hearing Voices,
 Francis Had Six-Pack Abs / 2

Francis In Perugia / 3

Teen Age Jesus / 5

Cement At San Damiano / 6

Jesus Examines The Blueprints / 7

On A Night When The Town Sleeps
 Francis And Leo Are Taken
 By The Beauty Of The Moon / 8

After Being Transported In Time, Francis
 Rides With Clare On A Tandem Bicycle / 9

Satori In A Village In Old Mexico / 10

Grace / 11

Clare And Agnes In Joplin / 12

Francis Kisses A Leper / 14

Brother Masseo's GPS / 16

Ruffino And Francis Step-Off The Bus
 At A Major Shopping District / 18

Francis Shoots Pool At Chubb's Bar / 19

How Saint Anthony Converted The Heretics
 By Preaching To Fishes / 21

Brother Giles Beats Walnuts / 22

Brother Juniper's Weird Gift / 23
Brother Juniper's Weird Gift: Two / 25
Altar Bells / 26
The Naked Fool / 28
Brother Juniper Rides The See-Saw / 29
Juniper's Vision Of The Floating Hand / 30
Francis Responds To An Email From
   Brother Ruffino Who Is Plagued By A Slick
   Talking Horned Demon / 32
Fruit Flies / 34
Francis Sings In An Ozark Cave / 36
The Good Karma Stop Light / 39
New Beginning Car Wash / 41
Clare's Vision Of The Jam / 42
Stigmata / 45
St. Francis Borrows A Fishing Net / 47
Bradford Dillman In The Basement / 48
A Given Name / 50
Waiting On Lazarus / 52
After Hard Times, Lazarus Feels
   The Beginning Of Something Good / 54

This book is dedicated to the memory of my father
Alfred Francis Ortolani and to J.T. Knoll, aka, Father
Two Beavers, a voice crying in the wilderness

THURSDAY MORNING

Lazarus can't find his car keys.
He checks all of his pockets, his
book bag, the top of the counter
by the micro-wave. Jesus's meeting
with Caiaphas hangs in the balance
and if he doesn't get
to the temple on time, then
punctuality on all matters
of prophecy will be doubted.
His mother has gone shopping
for a shroud, his father is
occupied in heaven. His 12 BFFs
are making plans for the weekend,
starting with a bite at Arimathea's—
then a garden reception. Reluctantly, Jesus
walks to the bus stop where he buys
 a one way metro pass. The clerk behind
the counter won't meet his eye; a woman
in the back of the bus
weeps quietly into her hands.

BEFORE HEARING VOICES, FRANCIS HAD SIX-PACK ABS

Francis buys a leather jacket, one that fits
like soft denim, but in a brown lamb or calfskin.
It takes away all of his worries. As a new man,
he faces the changing seasons with confidence
and aplomb. He nurses a drink
while leaning on a bar rail, and lovely women
wonder what he ordered. Their husbands
study wardrobe, tug at their jacket sleeves.
His girl believes she is the most desirable
woman in the bar. She places her hand on his arm
where it remains for the entire evening.
He never takes the jacket off, except to shower.
It hangs on the hook for the towel.
He uses scented soap, probably Polo Black,
and medicated shampoo that reduces dandruff.
Each time he steps in front of the mirror—there's
the low BMI, the cut pectorals, the six-pack abs.
On the street, strangers
ask him for Brad Pitt's autograph.

FRANCIS IN PERUGIA

The Burlington Northern
drums through the intersection
in old town—running

night by night,
hour by hour, hefting
freight, hauling coal.

The engineer trombones
the diesel's passing, calling
to each whistle post

the rhythm of the throttle,
measure by measure,
crossing by crossing—

a horn in the faraway, a
blizzard in the wheels.
Lying feverish in his cell

miles from town, he
recalls the sparrow
in St. Bede's hall,

darting from storm to
warmth of the fire,
the long tables filled

with food and drink,
music, dance, then
flying out again

through winter's
door. What lies before
and what lies after

is darkness, a swooping
bird in the storm,
a blizzard in the wheels.

TEEN AGE JESUS

Jesus came home one afternoon
while his mother was cooking fish
she'd bought from the Simon Brothers.
Are you making plans for tonight
with that Magdalene girl? She asked.
Jesus shrugged, She's cute, mom,
but I think we're better off
just as friends. Besides,
I'm hanging with Lazarus tonight.
He's been in a dark place since Passover.
We're meeting cousin John
for locusts and honey. He knows a place
down by the river where
they serve them up on platters.

CEMENT AT SAN DAMIANO

If a bluebird lands on the slate roof,
Francis knows the voice
speaks from the Gospel. Three times

he opens the book. Three times
the bluebird sings.
The rest is conjecture, based

on a semaphore of wings
and flashing trowel, the flock gathering,
a church to be rebuilt.

Francis lifts the droll stone.
He taps it from the scaffold
into the cornice. His eyes

are clear. Cement is a gift
from the Romans, how odd to be
mixed with birdsong.

JESUS EXAMINES THE BLUEPRINTS

The wiry little carpenter with the pointed beard
digs into his tool belt for nails, slips
his pencil behind his ear. He'll work
Sundays if he has too, knowing well
the price of being underbid,
remodeling costs more per square foot
than any new spec house
but the old place is a mess. Peter suggests
a triplex. Judas a bulldozer.

As an independent contractor
he's got to start somewhere, if eventually
he wants to turn water into wine
and to divide the fish and the loaves
among the hungry. Then there's the matter
of the building permit. The city inspector.
The other guy who walks on water.

ON A NIGHT WHEN THE TOWN SLEEPS FRANCIS AND LEO ARE TAKEN BY THE BEAUTY OF THE MOON

Francis and Leo watch an old DVD
of *Moonstruck*. Later, Leo steps out
into the front yard. The same moon
that enchanted Cosmo in the movie,
rests on the roof of Madden's house.
He calls Francis and the two of them
walk the sleeping streets, moonlight
like a lake. The moon enters
without knocking. It unlatches
fastened windows. Together, they run
the sidewalk, shaking neighbor's cars.
Security alarms begin to ring
up and down Olive Street. Widow
Madden throws open her door
and aims her husband's .22 pistol.
Leo is dancing in her driveway.
Francis plays his imaginary violin, two
sticks crossing in the porch light.

AFTER BEING TRANSPORTED IN TIME, FRANCIS RIDES WITH CLARE ON A TANDEM BICYCLE

She's beautiful in her disinterest,
pedaling in time, muscled, unrelenting
in her power stroke, her eyes keen
on the narrow roadside
that shoulders into forest: buntings,
larks, common sparrows,
sassafras, scrub oak, willows
woven through fencerow.
He longs to turn his head, to watch
her animal breathing, her feral
attentiveness to blackberries
bloom and thorn. He tamed
the wolf of Gubbio: livestock
safe; village safe;
wolf apologetic. At dusk
they rest in the howl of Amarillo.
She sips from the water bottle—night hawks
diving through truck stop lights.

SATORI IN A VILLAGE IN OLD MEXICO

You ask me if I can smell the prayer in cooking
in the smoke of the sidewalk enchiladas,
grilled chicken, onions on charcoal.

I half expect to see Francis
hobbling across the plaza on bare feet, Clare beside him.
Their eyes somewhere off beyond the church

and the incredulous Brother Leo. Somewhere off
beyond the vows in the sunlight
where the song of the bluebird begins.

GRACE

The day the Messiah
came to dinner,
she set out the best china
and her wedding crystal.

When she asked Him to say grace,
He only smiled,
pointing to His mouthful
of mashed potatoes.

CLARE AND AGNES IN JOPLIN

Where her house stood is a wilderness of power
lines, concrete blocks, and roofing from the church.
Natural gas wheezes from brass hot water

tank couplings. Street water runs ankle deep from
curb to curb. She emerges from behind a curtain
of rain, a cat in the crook of her arm. She

flashes a smile at her father who is digging
through the rubble of her living room. He drops
his shovel and wipes the storm from his brow.

A second day of rain lashes the courtyard. A single
spike heel rests on a shard of plywood roofing.
Two firemen lift the section and peer below.

Where is the evening dress with the slender
shoulder straps, the sequenced clutch, the woman
who tenderly exposed her neck to the night?

They lift joist after joist. Aluminum flashing reflects
more lightning streaking the west.
Rescue rests on their pry bars. A dog team,

nosing below a recliner sofa, uncovers a nest
of squirrels, their bodies swollen, arms rigid,
straightened as if caught in the act of leaping.

Squawk of a police radio, across the litter of tree limbs,
looters are escorted from a doorway, first sun
handcuffed to their wrists. Clare and Agnes

pull a Radio Flyer down 26th Street, handing out hot
meals in Styrofoam. A mile across the debris field,
their own stove lies upended, buried with Sunday's

supper: pork roast, mashed potatoes, green beans,
peach cobbler for an uncle. Dish towels
buried under plaster. Forks driven through trees.

FRANCIS KISSES A LEPER

—after "Dios" by Cesar Vallejo

God is the orphan of the universe.
We put him on a shelf, isolated, apart
from the current of stars, the pin-

wheel of galaxies. He's a bit like
an old movie, maybe *King Kong*,
or better yet, *Harvey*, picked up

in VHS, probably at a garage sale.
We watch him when the mood
for popcorn strikes us. This is why

I kissed the leper, his crumbly lips,
missing ear, the rope of dead flesh
tied like a cincture around his

waist. Then too, *Ben Hur* was a
wonderful movie, his mother and sis-
ter lost to the Valley of Lepers. He

held them both in his arms, brought
them out into a different light. There
you have it in the church of Hollywood—

I could sit on the couch all night
buttered and salted like my
bowl of Orville Redenbacher.

BROTHER MASSEO'S GPS

Confused at the crossroads,
Francis suggests that Brother
Masseo twirl

like a child at play.
Masseo spins until his head
begins to swim. He grows

giddy and falls into the mud,
his body a compass,
needle pointing to Siena.

It appears brother, Francis observes,
a higher power has chosen
to splatter you

with direction. Preaching
to birds and rabbits,
the occasional squirrel,

is all well and fine. Even now,
it has stimulated a market
in concrete garden art.

Stomach churning, Masseo
asks Francis for a Dramamine.
Francis produces a lemon

and splitting it with his knife
suggests they suck on it
as they walk.

RUFFINO AND FRANCIS STEP-OFF THE BUS AT A MAJOR SHOPPING DISTRICT

Our message needs a new metaphor.
Must we preach naked again, Ruffino mutters.
Let's avoid cliches, Francis continues. No cardboard signs.

No drum circles. Saxophones are misunderstood.
We are not seeking our big break. No dancing
with finger cymbals. Let penance be subtle.

Ruffino sits on the curb and rubs his temples,
what to do what to do, he groans. Francis produces a tablet
of paper and a stub of charcoal. Try caricatures-

each man, each woman, draw them as beasts
with sharp canines, or as fowl, feathers daubed in shit.
Ruffino raises his palms, empty of understanding.

In their eyes, good brother, lighten the charcoal.
Reflect the season, the starting and stopping
of busses, the cough of diesel, the whine of speed.

FRANCIS SHOOTS POOL AT CHUBB'S BAR

Wednesday advertises half-price chili & 50 cent draws.
Frosted mugs for each draught. Juniper racks up the balls
under the low hanging Schlitz light. Francis chalks

his cue and watches the balls roll tight, black 8
nestled in the center like an egg. Mary Magdalene
sits at a high chair against the wall, explaining

the rules of cutthroat to John the Baptist. Brother Leo
slides a shuffle board puck across the sawdust.
His nonchalance suggests he is waiting for inspiration.

Eventually, the backdoor opens and a troupe of young
roughnecks enters from the alley. They push quarters
up on the table. Francis and Juniper partner up.

Francis lets the one they call Raymond break. He slops in
a couple of stripes, then scratches on the orange 13.
Juniper begins to run the table. Leo stops to watch, sidles

up to his odd friend and whispers in his ear. These guys
are trouble. You might want to let them win.
Juniper grins; I'm already playing left handed.

Francis orders a round of beers from Chubb
and hands one to the leader with the wolfish eyes.
Have you tried the chili? He asks. It's to die for.

HOW SAINT ANTHONY CONVERTED THE HERETICS BY PREACHING TO FISHES

Standing on the banks between the river
and the sea, Anthony began to call the fishes.
He must have admired their calm,

seeing how they rose to the surface,
eyes lucid as the water, swimming
with others of their kind, small fish

to the shallow water and larger fish
to the deeper. Look how they wait

a bit out of water like rows of piano keys,
stirred by their longing to be played,
each word a fingertip on the head of a fish.

See how they sink when touched,
a musical note dropping into the depths
to stir in quiet schools, listening.

BROTHER GILES BEATS WALNUTS

Already the poor are coming, they push
shopping carts and sling plastic bags
across their shoulders. Those with addresses

have food stamps, those without drag
cardboard boxes and scraps of blue tarp.
Beyond the trees, crows dot the cornfields.

Giles weaves baskets and trades them
to farmers for corn. Among the crows,
there is no concept of justice. Their wings

dot the fields. They eat everything they can,
pecking their way from fence to fence.
Giles wraps walnuts in his cloak.

He hands them out to the poor on the road.
They follow him like tame birds, all
a juggle of feather and bone.

BROTHER JUNIPER'S WEIRD GIFT

Your old friend at the Golden Age Home
has fallen ill—a shut in
who spends most of each day

waking from lozenges of sleep.
He dreams of eating pig's feet,
and upon waking can't shake his hunger,

fried, pickled, smoked,
salted like bacon.
As a do-gooder (you), find

a shoat in the fields, lasso him
beside the stone fence and hogtie him
with hemp rope. You axe

one foot (the pig's), leaving him
to squeal, terrorized in the after-
noon sun. Then all hell breaks loose,

the farmer, crazed by your stupidity,
seeks answers, coins, apology. You claim
God's voice (the He), blind faith, an

ingenuous mercy. Even Francis, doves
on his shoulders, hare in the crook
of his arm is aghast. You ask the farmer

for forgiveness, the pig limping
towards supper (his last). The missing foot
gone on ahead (somewhere).

BROTHER JUNIPER'S WEIRD GIFT: TWO

You do your part to look the fool. Who
will deny you that, Brother Juniper? Look today
how the frost fingers the rocks, glazes

the milkweed, breaks with the tread
of your scampy shoes. You dance and whirl
through the city streets the same as you do

the back woods, fierce with conflict,
stippled with contradiction. Does the hawk
love the field mouse? Do you cry

for slaughtered pigs? You are the honest clown,
your humor like sleet. Pines twist into sun.
When morning finally crests the trees,

your tracks will have melted into mud.
All that is hoary will have grayed—so brief
is insight, so short-sighted the day.

ALTAR BELLS

A woman begs bus fare,
her cardboard placard creased
and stained. The penniless Juniper

asks her to wait while he ducks
into the church. He returns
with bells in a paper bag.

Silver is better pawned, he tells her.
The police usher Juniper
into the station where he

confesses eventually, seeming
to enjoy the good cop,
bad cop. The sergeant shouts

until his voice cracks. Later
that night, Juniper wakes the cop
at his home, flashlight in hand,

soup steaming in a plastic bowl.
Your voice box is injured
from yelling, he says.

This soup, my mother's
recipe, will calm
the wolf in your throat.

The sergeant is furious.
Do you know what time it is?
To which Juniper replies—

if you're not interested,
then at least hold my light
so I can eat. The sergeant

rubs his hand through his hair,
letting the door swing open.

THE NAKED FOOL

Once again Juniper is naked. The police
corner him in an alley just off 13th
and Baltimore. He has ignored the judge

and given his clothes away. This time
he insists is different. The man was shivering,
squatting on the steam grate like a Buddha—

the theft mutually agreed upon.

Pigeons fight for space on window sills
and the wind curls the exhaust of taxis
into gray winter snakes. The officer drapes

a blanket over Juniper's shoulders.
The lights on Baltimore flip to red—darkness
is the pocket change of night, the cold

its hard currency. There is plenty of both.
Juniper is a fool, already he is planning
how to lose the new blanket.

BROTHER JUNIPER RIDES THE SEE-SAW

Not as simple as it seems, balancing
a 2 x 6 on a guard rail, two boys
on one end, a skinny monk
on the other, the three riding, wildly happy.
The elders emerge at the city gates,
walking their coifed spaniels. They are
curious and wish to show
the celebrity monk through the streets,
display him on Channel 5 News.
Juniper refuses their intentions,
keeps to the see-saw, rocking
higher and faster. The boys laugh,
shouting for more. Finally, a rumor
spreads among the crowd— the holy man
is a nut case, daft as a drumstick.
Juniper breathes easier,
the boys beat their fists, the plank
rises higher, even the sparrows
are crazy for more.

JUNIPER'S VISION OF THE FLOATING HAND

Brother Juniper has been praying for days—
What else? It's his mojo, you know, these
crazy acts of devotion. One afternoon

a floating hand appears out of the blue.
It's like some kind of *You Are Here* sign—
disembodied, unadorned by rings

or jewels of office. It's as plain to see
as a pig ballooned in sunlight. Juniper
appears to be the only one who has noticed

and he turns circles, but the friars are doing
their own prayer jumbo (gesticulating,
flagellating). Out of the woods, a voice

speaks into his ear, *There is nothing
you can do with this hand.*
Juniper isn't so sure, he shakes himself

as if brushing leaves, acorns—second
thoughts from his tunic. He walks
among the mendicants, encouraging

himself to do nothing. This is difficult—
certainly a let go and let God
type of moment—the oaks stirring

with sunlight, the road to town
no busier than usual—God's hand
in high definition.

FRANCIS RESPONDS TO AN EMAIL FROM BROTHER RUFFINO WHO IS PLAGUED BY A SLICK TALKING HORNED DEMON

Francis clicks *Reply
to all*—
this devil (as many

hold stock), lays
province to the wheat fields
as much as the city.

He doesn't fear
the fundamentalists—
he bullshits for corn,

beans, wheat. He is
comfortable with single
issue politics, avoids

critical thinking, turns
your words to turds. Our demon
breeds myopia & displays

a lack of humor. He
bides his time, sharpening
lawn mower blades,

spitting tobacco juice,
thumping the bejesus
out of his Bible.

It's all just slick talk—
if he opens his mouth again—
shit down his throat.

FRUIT FLIES
for Trout

After the stroke, Elias
ate better, salmon for supper,
salad for lunch, almonds

between meals. He limited
his drinking to red wine
from a gallon jug. He seldom

touched the stuff until
late in the afternoon. At
Pollo's Market he

shopped for fruit. The walk
up the Boulevard did him
good. He returned relaxed,

slicing an apple with his
pen knife, doling out cherries
from a brown sack. Mostly,

Elias enjoyed the sun, as it
bent over the Sangre
De Christos, the blood of Christ

like a pomegranate. He emailed
Francis from the library—
the price of lemons

peaks at a dollar, fat, slick-
skinned, as crisp
as prescription pads. Obama

better hurry. Tomorrow
I hear they charge for sunlight,
even the fruit flies pay.

FRANCIS SINGS IN AN OZARK CAVE

I.

Francis sings Amazing Grace in an Ozark cave.
He likes the acoustics of emptiness, the chance
to sing to the unseen, to hear
each note with crisp edges, uncluttered.

Elias is always the Boy Scout: three
sources of light, a trash bag, water, granola.
If lost, turned sideways, confused by
passage imitating passage—he slits the bag, slips it

over his head, and sits cross-legged—the plastic
pulled down to his knees—the candle
nursed between his legs like tea.

II.

Francis searches the source of breeze
in his face—new cave, wiggle room, a squeeze.
Darkness becomes personal, more pressing—
scalloped walls curving on. The belay
of his voice is roped through the loneliness
like a bowline at his waist. When Elias leaves
work on Monday, he is off-rope, the Boy Scout
heading home, briefcase topped

with chemistry, valence bonding, compound
to compound. He walks the snowmelt
to his silver Nissan, gray

III.

drifts thawing into creeks. At the storm drain,
the run-off sluices through concrete
to a distant spillway. This too is cave,
hypothermic, piped beneath the streets

like a subterranean piano—key by key, note by note.
He listens to public radio on the drive
across Kansas City. A Lexus swings
into the passing lane. The driver has a clipboard

on the steering wheel. He gestures wildly
into his Bluetooth. All the way to the exit
on 435—his hands fly like bats.

THE GOOD KARMA STOP LIGHT

I'm thinking of St. Francis and the lepers
when this one legged panhandler
hops into the traffic. He holds

out his hand— *I'm selling
good karma man.* The light is red.
No way to kick

the gas pedal and skirt
the intersection. Sherri is Sister Clare
rolling down her window

digging through her purse.
She has a few twenties and a couple
of ones. I say give him a dollar.

The one legged man, balanced like
a pogo stick—the bus to good karma
costs more than a buck. She slips

a twenty through the window.
The light changes and I gas it
across Congress. In the rearview

the beggar bounces back
to his bus stop—the twenty
flapping like a prayer flag.

NEW BEGINNING CAR WASH

At the New Beginning Car Wash, Mary and Joseph
look for a spot free rinse for their old Pontiac.
It's a rust bucket

straight from a Judean low-credit lot.
One owner the salesman had said and Joseph
had bartered and haggled and then paid

in hard earned carpenter's wages.
He had to get his family to Egypt— for danger
was in the air and angels were rattling his dreams.

It is a dusty drive he was thinking
and we are in such a press what with all this Herod trouble.
Of course, a car that's newly washed

won't run any better than a dirty one,
but the white walls when scrubbed will look
like halos in the sun spinning across the Sinai.

CLARE'S VISION OF THE JAM

I.

Francis plays his invisible sax; Leo stomps
like a dervish. Wild onions swell in bulbs
at their feet. Each morning is balanced on

the cusp of wildness. All night the creaking
cold tumbles on the wind, the wolf
in the trees. When every coat is given away,

there are just the stones, the breath
freezing in scat. Melody teeters between
madness and vision, between blood and bone—

Francis flexes his fingers on the keys.
Already Gene Krupa's crazy

II.

drumsticks beat the skull. Each new day
is an improvisation—a jazz riff. One long jam
session with clarinets, toms, and horns. Unable

to leave her bed, Clare begins to hum
the tune. She breaks bread with the forest—
click of willow above the stream, snare

of fish at her feet, sparrows like quarter notes.
The stones of her cell pixelate in high definition,
the entire wall a flat screen. Francis

is with Leo on the bandstand. Clare drums
the mattress, watches from afar.

III.

In 1958 Clare is named the patroness
of television. Ozzie and Harriet plan
Sunday dinner. Paladin hands out

business cards. Kookie Kookson
combs his hair on Sunset Strip.
Poor Clare, too sick to leave her cell,

watches the stones glow with excitement,
dried yarrow, juniper, stars above
the thatch, geese on the wind. A family

in Kansas City shares popcorn on the couch.
Ed Sullivan introduces Topo Gigio.

STIGMATA

Each morning you will rise
before the sun. It will fling
its rays over the horizon like ropes

and you will be expected
to climb them. Each day
you will be understood less.

How can it be otherwise,
touched as you are? In preparation
you will not sleep. Black bread

holds you like a stone. Soup itself
is a sandbag. Each night
you will wait through the hours

for the first movement of the sun
as it grinds upwards. Even those
who tell your story will be

suspect—each revision an attempt
to get the story. You will be
watched like a magician

with a deck of cards—show us
how you pulled the ace—local
television will have a chopper

ready to broadcast
whatever happens next. Let us
give this up, Leo says. The woods

are complete with miracles.
Sparrows soar.

ST. FRANCIS BORROWS A FISHING NET

In each cast, the fisherman drags the shoal
for shad. They tail-spin out of the water, slap

the current. Trolling hand over hand, Francis
feeds them into the bait bucket at his feet.
The empty net is thrown in an upward motion

to fan the shallows, the shad like skipping rocks,
like silver in the deep pool. Francis swings
the empty net—the green river running

through the night. The current billows and sinks
the woven hemp in his hands, his knotted forearms,
his bloodied wrists. Fish swim through centuries—

as timeless as hunger.

BRADFORD DILLMAN IN THE BASEMENT

When I was a kid, I watched
Bradford Dillman as St. Francis
on the television. Dad was

refinishing the basement
while I sat on the floor touched
in the sawdust by the old

black and white. I cried
in the newness, spreading
my arms on the bathroom tile

between the sink and the bi-fold doors.
I used Dillman's lines
and prayed for the blood.

Years later, I visited Assisi
to say a rosary for my father
who had grown old with his basement

and who was now—new to death.
Sequestered in a back pew,
I hid my tears from the other tourists,

beads clacking, nothing black,
nothing white.
Few knew my father as a bird watcher,

his chair by the back porch
positioned so he could keep his eyes
on the feeders and the martin house.

In summer sparrows slipped
through the open doors of the Basilica.
The drumming of their wings

like voices, distant, removed.

A GIVEN NAME

Hey Lou! watched television at Chubb's.
He spoke when spoken to
in soft syllables that seldom

crossed the bar. He measured the night
with quart beer, glasses of Schlitz
topped with tomato juice.

I knew the house he returned to—
delivered his groceries as a boy. Hey Lou!
let me in through the kitchen,

the light to the clock above the stove
always blue. He kept a photograph
of a woman on the dining table. I imagined

the two of them eating together. More
than his given name between them. Hey Lou!
raised canaries, heated his garage—

insulated it with thin visqueen plastic.
Above the barrels of birdseed
was a cheap litho of Saint Francis

blessing the turtle doves.

Hey Lou! shoveled the snow,
waved to the neighbors—spread
rock salt along the sidewalk.

WAITING ON LAZARUS

I dream of my father as Lazarus
come back from the dead. He is
weaker though, somehow still

sick with the cancer. His time
is counted in days that he manages
to extend to weeks, even months.

We go about family business,
lunches on Sunday, grandchildren
splashing in the above ground.

The carpeted deck alive
with flowers and sun. Yet, still
there is a grayness to it, knowing

that he faces the end again. The grief
keeps recycling, each dream
as predictable as the last.

We know to gather, telling the same
jokes by his bed, monitors bleeping
like winter birds. When the tubes

are removed, dangling to the floor
like extension cords, I climb
onto a chair in the waiting room

and disconnect the fluorescent
bulbs, finding the dimness
that I need to close my eyes,

my sister pillowed on the couch,
arm across her face, shutting out
the glare, the shine of the wait.

AFTER HARD TIMES, LAZARUS FEELS THE BEGINNING OF SOMETHING GOOD

He has driven all night
and can find no rest. He thinks
of himself as Lazarus risen
but not quite alive,

calls himself that name
in idle conversations with the windshield,
poems to the radio knobs that glow
in green iridescence.

He has crossed Kansas in rain
and with dawn is steering into the
watery veins of eastern fields.
Any moment, the sun

will drop a single rope
from between blue clouds, and he
will dance on the wet highway
like a child whose guardian angel

has slipped from heaven and perched
like a yellow bird on the bedstead,
meadowlarks rising from fence posts.

www.ingramcontent.com/pod-product-compliance
Lightning Source LLC
Chambersburg PA
CBHW030133100526
44591CB00009B/635